Presented To:

_____

From:

_____

Date:

_____

How to Become Debt $FREE

HONOR [HB] BOOKS

Inspiration and Motivation for the Seasons of Life

COOK COMMUNICATIONS MINISTRIES
Colorado Springs, Colorado • Paris, Ontario
KINGSWAY COMMUNICATIONS LTD
Eastbourne, England

Honor® is an imprint of
Cook Communications Ministries, Colorado Springs, CO 80918
Cook Communications, Paris, Ontario
Kingsway Communications, Eastbourne, England

POCKET PLAN™: BECOMING DEBT-FREE
© 2005 by Honor Books

First Printing, 2005
Printed in Canada

Printing/Year
1 2 3 4 5 6 7 8 9 10 / 10 09 08 07 06 05

ISBN: 1562927345

"Pay every debt, as if God wrote the bill."

RALPH WALDO EMERSON

"There can be no freedom or beauty about a home life that depends on borrowing or debt."

HENRIK IBSEN

Sara: "What would you do if you had all the money in the world?"

Sam: "I'd apply it to my debts, as far as it would go."

"IF ONLY I COULD GET OUT OF DEBT…"

Do you feel like Sam? That your debts are mounting faster than your ability to pay them? That "if only you could get out of debt," you could do so many good things such as:

- save more for retirement,
- handle your next financial emergency with cash,
- save and pay cash for your vacation or next car,
- give more to charity or ministry, and
- feel financially free—at last?

Like most good things in life, credit is meant to be used wisely, not abused. It can be a valuable asset if we respect it for what it is: a tool to help us acquire appreciating items such as a home, investment real estate, or a promising business.

But where many good people get into trouble is with the use of *consumer credit*: those credit cards, charge cards, loans-by-mail or e-mail, and even home equity loans that are used for *perishable* or *depreciating* items.

TAKIN' IT TO THE STREET

The average American family holds credit-card and charge-card debt of more than $8,200 on 16 (!) credit cards or charge cards. And this does not include the non-plastic notes we owe on cars, trucks, SUVs, RVs, ATVs, or other acronymic toys that spill from our jammed garages onto our driveways or streets.

"Men may not get all they pay for in this world, but they must certainly pay for all they get."

FREDERICK DOUGLASS

"There was a time when a fool and his money were soon parted, but now it happens to everybody."

ADLAI E. STEVENSON

"Beware, and be on your guard
against every form of greed…

...for not even when one has
an abundance does his life consist
of his possessions."

LUKE 12:15 NASB

"**W**e'll show the world we're prosperous even if we have to go broke to do it."

WILL ROGERS

CREDIT 'N' STUFF

Consumer credit, and the ease with which we can attain and use it, has created a dilemma:

On the one hand, we want to look and feel financially successful, so we want the Stuff we think financially successful people should have. Saving for it takes too long because we want to look and feel successful *now*. So we whip out the plastic so we can take our Stuff home today.

But on the other hand, a funny thing happens as we accumulate the Stuff we think will help us feel good: We find ourselves caught in a revolving door of debt.

The Stuff that was such a "must buy" isn't nearly as fascinating several weeks after the purchase, and the monthly payments continue unabated—with interest! Our "must buys" all become "must pays."

So to service the debt, we must shortchange either our present or our future. We're paying for yesterday's purchases, which means less money for today's needs and tomorrow's dreams. Instead of financial freedom, we're in financial bondage. Which doesn't feel good at all, does it?

Consumer debt does not help you get ahead; it holds you back.

SOUND FAMILIAR?

Dear Ms. Smith:

Congratulations! You have been SPECIALLY SELECTED and PRE-QUALIFIED for the prestigious FutureShock Credit Card. Imagine the thrill of finally booking that dream vacation...

IN CASE OF EMERGENCY...

People rarely acquire credit cards intent on spending them into the stratosphere. The usual rationale for the first card or two is that "it'll be good to have for emergencies." But then... "emergencies" happen. Like an emergency dinner out. An emergency pair of shoes (and matching belt, of course). An emergency vacation. And the emergency Christmas that comes at the same time each year.

Besides, you'll pay off the full amount when the credit-card statement arrives, right?

Right.

Before that statement comes, another emergency is going to happen. (Count on it, like death and taxes.) Could be an emergency DVD or DVD player, or some fun computer software. You know, emergency Stuff.

NO WONDER THEY CALL IT "REVOLVING CREDIT"

So your statement arrives and your balance is now too high to pay in full. *I'll make the minimum payment this month, then pay it off next month*, you assure yourself.

And so it goes. Before you know it, you're trapped in the revolving door—paying heavily for your past and at horrific rates of interest to boot. Your monthly cash flow is strained, tempting you to use the card even more—perhaps even for normal monthly expenses that you formerly paid with cash.

"If the shoe fits, charge it."

ANONYMOUS*

*No one was willing to claim this pithy proverb, though we suspect
that you may know rather well the person who said it.

23

TOP 10 RATIONALIZATIONS FOR CREDIT-CARD SPENDING

The human being can be pretty creative when thinking up reasons to use and misuse those credit cards. Even when attempting to escape the revolving door you may catch yourself reverting to some wonderful-sounding explanations. See if you recognize any of the following Top 10 Rationalizations for Credit-Card Spending.

Number 10...

"I owe it to myself."

26

Number 9...

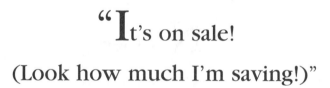

"It's on sale!

(Look how much I'm saving!)"

Number 8…

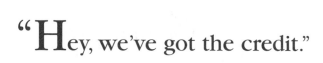

"Hey, we've got the credit."

Number 7...

"I don't have the cash on me, but I need this now."

32

Number 6...

"We'll pay it off with our tax refund."

Number 5…

"Web sites take only credit cards."

Number 4...

"QVC takes only credit cards."

Number 3...

"Now that we're becoming debt free we can splurge a little."

Number 2...

"God told me to buy it."

42

And the Number 1 Rationalization
for Credit-Card Spending…

"We'll pay it off this month. Or next."

44

"The borrower is servant to the lender."

PROVERBS 22:7 NIV

TRAPPED IN THE REVOLVING DOOR?

Has debt got you running in circles?

Have you become a "servant to the lender"?

Let's find out...

Your **honest answers** to the following 8 questions will help reveal if consumer debt is preventing you from addressing important financial priorities in your life...

1. Do my consumer debts (all debts other than home mortgages) total more than 5 percent of my gross annual income?

❑ Yes   ❑ No

Get out your most recent credit and installment card statements, car payment information, and any other documents showing what you presently owe for items or expenses which have *been consumed* (i.e. vacation, food, gasoline) or are *depreciating* in value (everything other than real estate mortgages or investment in a growing business). Now add all your current balances. The sum is your *total consumer debt.* (Your calculator may not have enough digits to display this sum.)

Take your total consumer debt and divide it by your gross annual income. **If the result is more than 5 percent, consumer debt is playing too big a role in your financial life**. We want to bring your outstanding consumer debt to zero and keep it there.

**2. Do I consistently pay only the
minimum amount due
each month on installment
or credit card purchases?**

☑ Yes   ☐ No

Your paying only the minimum amount due is **how creditors make big money**. *Your* **money**. It's in their best interest that you pay them as little as possible for as long as possible. They want the power of compound interest to work in *their* favor, not yours. Any time you let interest accrue on consumer debt by not paying in full, **you are allowing compound interest to work against you**—at the profit of your creditors.

3. Do I tend to add more expenses to an account than I can pay off at the end of the same month?

❑ Yes   ❑ No

If you add $125 in charges this month and pay only $50 when your statement arrives, you've carried $75 over into next month—on top of the existing balance. Meanwhile, the total carryover accrues interest, bringing you an even larger balance next month. Continue this practice and the revolving door speeds up. Do it with several accounts at once, as does the typical American family, and you're running in circles to keep from getting run over.

Ever tried to exit a fast-revolving door? There's only one way to do it safely: Stop pushing and slow it down gradually. You can escape consumer debt in the same way—stop pushing up your balances and systematically pay down your accounts.

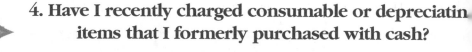

**4. Have I recently charged consumable or depreciatin
items that I formerly purchased with cash?**

☐ Yes ☐ No

Meals out, vacations, gasoline, oil and lube services, clothing, or anything that is consumed or depreciates in value should be purchased with cash. Do not put such items on credit unless you have the firm resolve and discipline to pay these charges in full when the statement arrives. Most people don't have this discipline unless the sum of such purchases is very low. So why tempt yourself? Just two or three of these modest expenditures can add up.

5. Do I have an inner "lack of peace" about my consumer-debt situation?

❏ Yes   ❏ No

If you've been fighting that "gotta get out of debt" feeling or have experienced anxiety over your financial obligations, you are experiencing financial bondage instead of financial freedom. Financial freedom means you are no longer cheating your future to pay for your past. It's the wonderful peace of mind that comes from being able to save and give more consistently because you've kept your spending and consumer debt under control.

6. Have I received any late-payment penalties, or letters or phone calls about late payments?

❑ Yes ❑ No

Late payments are a sure sign that excess commitments are forcing you to juggle your cash flow. Recent studies show that two-thirds of U.S. banks will raise your rates—as high as 29 percent—after only one late payment. And this is on top of late-payment fees averaging $35 per hit. Blow it just once or twice and your credit report will brand you as tardy, meaning higher interest rates when you truly need a "healthy" loan for your next home, continuing education, or business.

7. Am I unable to consistently put at least 10 percent of my gross annual income toward long-term savings and investment?

❑ Yes   ❑ No

A long-term savings strategy in which you save a minimum of 10 percent of your gross income is foundational to financial freedom. Saving less than that keeps you from building a healthy "cushion" for emergencies, a college fund for a growing child, and your personal retirement fund. If debt payments are forcing you to cheat your savings program, then your consumer debt is too high.

8. Am I unable to consistently give generously to my church and to other ministries, charities, or individuals in need?

❑ Yes ❑ No

"**H**onor the Lord from your wealth, and from the *first* of all your produce," counsels Proverbs 3:9 (NASB, emphasis added). Jesus himself taught, "Give and it will be given to you. A good measure, pressed down, shaken together and running over, will be poured into your lap. For with the measure you use, it will be measured to you" (Luke 6:38 NIV).

One cannot possibly enjoy financial freedom without first giving away a generous portion of his or her income. If you're unable to give consistently, it's a sure sign that your spending and consumer debt need to be brought under control.

If You Answered "Yes" . . .

If you answered Yes to any of the preceding questions, it's possible you have allowed the "buy now, pay forever" syndrome to trap you in consumer debt's revolving door. **If so, you're making your present financial life much tougher than necessary**. (It's no fun being "servant to the lender.")

You're *definitely* **compromising your future financial strength** by using today's dollars to pay for things that happened weeks, months, or years ago. Perhaps most seriously, your finances may actually be in jeopardy without a swift and sure mid-course correction.

But please don't despair—people in far worse shape have become debt-free, and so can you. And it's going to feel so good!

"Compensatory Consumption"

Two British researchers took an academic look in 2000 at why we go shopping. They believe that when we shop for anything other than the true basics, it's because we're missing something else in our lives. The catch phrase for this behavior is called "retail therapy," but in academic circles it's called "compensatory consumption."

JEAN CHATZKY

Pay It Down!

"If you find yourself in a hole,
the first thing to do is stop digging."

WILL ROGERS

Turnaround Day!

Take a moment to review your answers to the eight questions on the preceding pages. If you answered "Yes" to any of them, you're either flirting with trouble or you've already found it. But you're going to change that—beginning today!

Mark this day on your calendar: *Turnaround Day*. Today is the day you begin to slow the revolving door and regain control of your personal finances. When you put this proven Pocket Plan to work, here's what's going to happen...

First, you're going to GAIN CONTROL OF YOUR CASH FLOW.

When you no longer have to service those enslaving monthly debt payments, you'll have more money to enjoy life *now*, to handle emergencies with cash, to save and invest for the future, and to give to your church or favorite charities.

Second, you'll STOP COMPOUND INTEREST FROM WORKING AGAINST YOU and get it working for you.

 Eliminate a 16 percent debt and your immediate return-on-investment is 16 percen (Talk about a sure thing!) Redirect those debt-payment dollars to savings and investme and interest will start working for you instead of against you.

Third, you'll begin to FEEL FINANCIALLY FREE!

No longer will you feel like a "slave to the lender," making endless payments on depreciating or already-consumed purchases. Peace of mind is one of the best investments you'll ever make.

And fourth, you'll be able to
MAKE FUTURE PURCHASES WITH CASH.

When there's a genuine need or you just want to do something fun, you'll pay with cash instead of plastic. With a rejuvenated savings program, the funds will be there for you—designated for just such an event. You won't spend months or years and countless interest dollars paying for your purchase after it's consumed or stored away. You will be "in charge" instead of the lender charging *you*.

Of the average American's take-home pay, 23 percent is already committed to repayment of existing debt.

REPORTED BY BETHANY AND SCOTT PALMER

Cents & Sensibility

Perception of Prosperity

"**C**redit cards give the perception of prosperity but the reality of impoverishment. The innocent-appearing plastic card draws its life from our financial margin, becoming more powerful as we sink deeper into debt. Soon we find ourselves looking up from a deep hole, surrounded by possessions we do not really own."

RICHARD A. SWENSON, M.D.

Margin

"There is an opportunity cost to consumption. A dollar spent today does *not* take a dollar out of the future; it takes *multiple* dollars."

RON BLUE

Master Your Money

The 10 Simple Secrets to Becoming Debt-Free

"Neither a borrower nor a lender be;
For loan oft loses both itself and a friend."

WILLIAM SHAKESPEARE

HAMLET

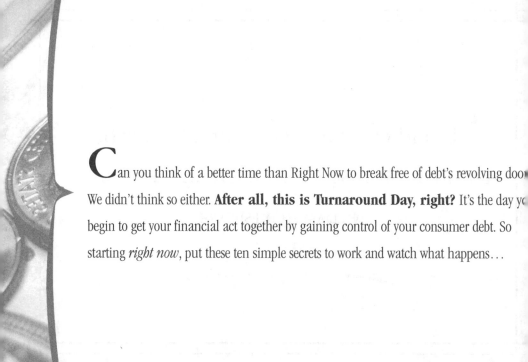

Can you think of a better time than Right Now to break free of debt's revolving door? We didn't think so either. **After all, this is Turnaround Day, right?** It's the day you begin to get your financial act together by gaining control of your consumer debt. So starting *right now*, put these ten simple secrets to work and watch what happens...

"A creditor is worse than a master,
for a master owns only your person;
a creditor owns your dignity and can
belabour that."

VICTOR HUGO

Les Miserables

1. MAKE THE COMMITMENT: NO NEW CONSUMER DEBT.

Boldly. Irrevocably. Other than your home mortgage (which in most cases is an appreciating asset), your goal is to eliminate all consumer debt and turn those debt-servicing dollars into YOU-servicing dollars. From this day forward, you're going to cease cheating your future to pay for your past. You're going to operate pay-as-you-go, cash only.

We know it sounds melodramatic, but you gotta do it. An alcoholic, for example, can't just "taper off" or enjoy a drink here and there. He must stop—completely— and imbibe NO alcohol if he wants to stop harming himself and others.

Here's a **"simply powerful" tip to help you:** Whenever you find yourself adding an impulse item to your cart or whipping out the plastic for an in-store, online, or telephone purchase, ask yourself: *"REALLY?"* As in, do you *REALLY* need what you're about to purchase? (Ninety-nine times out of a hundred, the correct answer is "No.") If you're married, promise each other that you'll pose the *"REALLY?"* challenge aloud any time the other is inclined to use a credit card. More often than not you'll place the item back on the shelf—even sheepishly—but you'll sleep better at night.

"REALLY?"

(Correct answer: "No.")

2. REDUCE YOUR CARD COLLECTION TO ONE CARD ONLY.

Just as an ex-smoker courts disaster if she keeps packs of cigarettes around the house, you risk blowing it if you hold too many credit cards. Keep in mind that behind every card lurks a financial institution that, frankly my dear, doesn't give a darn if you're dogpaddling in debt.

In fact, **these kindly institutions encourage you to charge everything** from diapers to doggy day care. They want you to accrue as much debt as possible so they'll earn heaps of interest on what they hope will be a v-e-r-y s-l-o-w payback on your part.

You simply do not need the motive nor the means that multiple cards give you to plunge deeper into debt. **Let's face it: The temptation is just too great.** It's too easy to justify excessive spending by saying, "It's okay, we have the credit."

Today, retake control of your credit by narrowing the total of your credit and charge cards to One Card Only. **Select the no-annual-fee credit card with the lowest interest rate** and set it aside for now. (This is the one and only card you're going to keep for a genuine caught-in-the-boondocks emergency.) Then (are you ready for some fun?) take the other cards— every single one of them—insert between scissors, and make confetti.

That's right, slice away. Sure, it hurts a little—just as it hurts when the doctor slices a cancerous growth from your body. But you're so much healthier afterwards! **You do not need these cards**. You're going to pay them off, close these accounts, and simplify your financial life by owning just one credit card. When debt's under control, why would you need more?

"The wicked borrows and
does not pay back,
But the righteous is gracious and gives."

PSALM 37:21 NASB

86

"When a man is in love or in debt, someone else has the advantage."

BILL BALNCE

3. REMOVE TEMPTATION FROM YOUR WALLET.

Okay, you're down to One Card Only. You're keeping it only for a genuine emergency. (Note to self: Mall crawling and Christmas shopping are not emergencies). you've indeed struggled with impulse spending, you'll now want to make this card mor difficult to access by keeping it out of sight and out of mind, in a place that forces you **pose the *REALLY?* challenge**.

How about keeping this card in a safe deposit box at the bank or, as several successful debt-busters have done, in a water-filled milk carton in your freezer. You'll be amazed how the spending urge passes after a couple of hours of thaw time! This secret **helps you stand strong in your commitment** to live pay-as-you-go instead of pay-as-you-went.

4. IN PLACE OF A CREDIT CARD, USE A DEBIT CARD.

Debit cards look and act much the same as a credit card but with one wonderful difference: If you put an expense on a debit card, it is automatically deducted from you checking account. Thus it draws from your cash, not your credit, and does not accrue interest or add to your debt.

Just about any place that takes credit cards takes debit cards, including online, mail, or phone sellers. Rare exceptions may include some car-rental agencies and hotels. Of course, when using the debit card **you'll need to be certain that**: (1) you have enough funds in checking to cover the expense; (2) you deduct the expense from your checking ledger immediately so it won't surprise you when the statement arrives; and (3) it's an expense your spending plan allows.

5. MAKE A "HIT LIST" OF ALL YOUR CREDITORS.

Don't worry, this isn't your usual hit list. The only crime you're going to commit is that of robbing your ravenous creditors of interest. Write down each creditor's name, the balance you owe, the interest rate, and the minimum monthly payment.

"**W**hatever you earn, spend less."

SAMUEL JOHNSON

6. PRIORITIZE YOUR HIT LIST FOR PAYDOWN.

You are going to **pick off your creditors one at a time** while keeping the others happy. So look over your Hit List and determine which creditor you'd like to pay first, second, third, and so on.

Financial advisors usually suggest that you pay down your most expensive debts first—those that cost you the most in monthly interest. From a purist's perspective this makes the most sense. However, because personal finance is as much psychological as it is financial, others find that debt busters do best if they target their smallest balances first. Paying off a creditor and crossing him off the list provides **a big psychological and emotional boost**, which makes you even more resolute. The quicker you can cross some debts off your list as Paid in Full, the more momentum and motivation you'll gain in your quest to become debt-free.

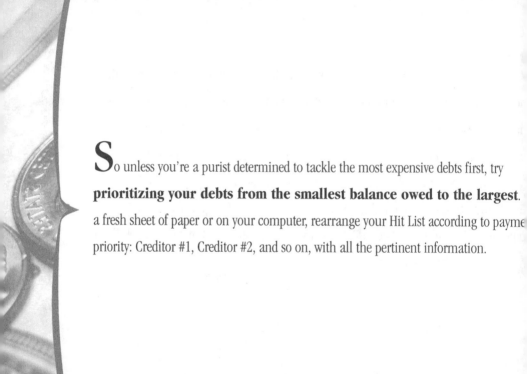

So unless you're a purist determined to tackle the most expensive debts first, try **prioritizing your debts from the smallest balance owed to the largest**. a fresh sheet of paper or on your computer, rearrange your Hit List according to payme priority: Creditor #1, Creditor #2, and so on, with all the pertinent information.

Go for the low-hanging fruit first.

7. SELL SOMETHING THIS WEEKEND.

Huh? That's right. There's no better way to jump-start a debt-busting program than **a quick infusion of cold, hard cash**. And you can probably find some quick cash in all the Stuff you've accumulated over the years.

What do you have sitting around that you can sell? (Okay, other than the husband.) How about an extra vehicle, or a motorcycle, bike, camera, computer, skis, tools, or exercise equipment? **All of us have too much Stuff—things that at one point we thought we *REALLY* needed**. They may as well be cluttering someone else's house, right? A weekend yard sale or eBay auction can turn your has-beens into ready cash which you can devote to debt elimination.

She makes linen garments and sells them,
And supplies belts to the tradesmen.

PSALM 31:24 NASB

Once you sell something, **turn right around, *same day*, and write a check** in the amount of your new-found money to Creditor #1. *If* you happen to raise enough cash to pay him off entirely (it could happen!) then apply the remaining found-cash to Creditor #2, and so on. More about this in step eight.

You're on the way to debt-freedom!

8. ASSIGN A MONTHLY PAYMENT TO EACH CREDITOR.

$\mathbf{B}$y now you've prioritized your creditors from smallest balance owed to largest, note their minimum required monthly payment, raised cash by selling some sins of your pa and sent the proceeds to Creditor #1. Here's how to proceed from here...

With the exception of Creditor #1, you're going to pay each creditor his monthly minimum only. Your top priority, Creditor #1, will receive his **required monthly minimum _plus_ an additional sum every month** until he's paid in full. Depending on your situation, your goal should be to **send at least $30 over and above Creditor #1's minimum payment**. Send more, much more, whenever you can so you can "knock him off" as quickly as possible.

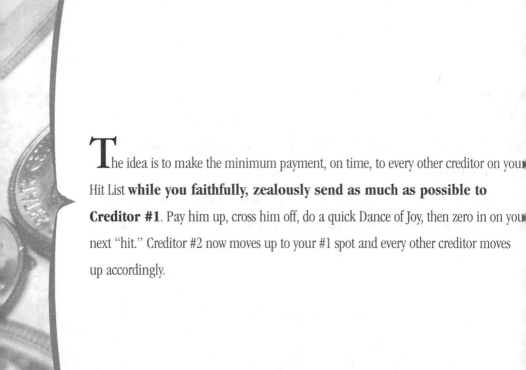

The idea is to make the minimum payment, on time, to every other creditor on your Hit List **while you faithfully, zealously send as much as possible to Creditor #1**. Pay him up, cross him off, do a quick Dance of Joy, then zero in on your next "hit." Creditor #2 now moves up to your #1 spot and every other creditor moves up accordingly.

"Creditors are a superstitious sect, great observers of set days and times."

BENJAMIN FRANKLIN

9. MAKE EACH PAYMENT FAITHFULLY AND ON TIME.

Never allow a payment to be late, and never, ever, make a creditor call you. As we'v already seen, the financial penalties for tardiness are steep. More importantly, **prompt payment is a matter of personal integrity**. You'll demonstrate good faith and f much better about yourself when you're diligent with every payment.

M̲ost credit card companies now allow you to pay by phone, so if you find yourself flirting with a deadline you can call and have a designated payment drafted from a checking or savings account. This service is also handy for making extra payments to Creditor #1 during the month so you won't have to hold cash for his next statement.

"**O**we nothing to anyone
except to love one another."

ROMANS 13:8 NASB

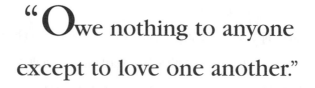

"Interest works night and day,
in fair weather and in foul.
It gnaws at a man's substance
with invisible teeth."

HENRY WARD BEECHER

Proverbs from Plymouth Pulpit

10. AS EACH DEBT IS ELIMINATED, SHIFT YOUR TOTAL MONTHLY PAYMENT FROM THE "ELIMINATED" CREDITOR TO THE NEXT CREDITOR ON YOUR HIT LIST.

If you've been behaving yourself, you turned all but one of your credit cards to confetti back in Step 2. This was to keep you from adding to those balances while you're paying them down. Hopefully, too, you've been standing strong against temptation to use your sole remaining credit card.

Now it starts to get fun because you're going to gang up on Creditor #1 until you've knocked him off. Once he's history, you'll re-deploy your resources to gang up on your next priority. And so on—until that wonderful day when you are finally debt-free.

Here's how it works. Say you've been making payments of $100 per month to Creditor #1, Wally's Wonder Wigs. Finally the blessed day arrives when you send Wally the final payment—Paid in Full! Now that your wigs are out of hock you'll **take that $100 per month and shift it to Creditor #2**, the prestigious platinum FutureShock credit card. This creditor now moves up to the #1 slot. Your minimum monthly payment to FutureShock had been $30, so your new monthly payment will now be $130. **(Send more if you receive extra cash during the month.)**

YES, YOU CAN!

In this day and age, disciplined debt elimination is not only counter-cultural, it's almost counter-intuitive. But freedom from consumer debt is foundational to financial success, so stand strong and work the plan. Of course, you can speed up Freedom Day by raising extra cash: Sell items you don't need, reduce "compensatory consumption," and consider some overtime or an extra, part-time job. Then direct the dollars you gain to your top-priority creditor.

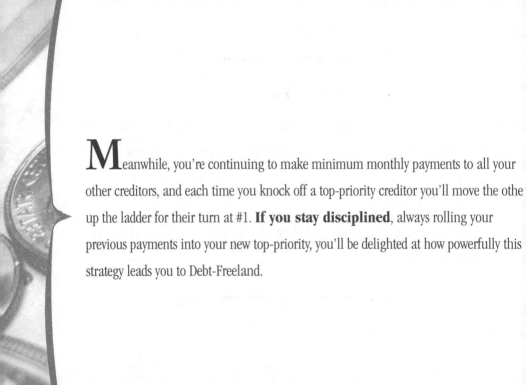

Meanwhile, you're continuing to make minimum monthly payments to all your other creditors, and each time you knock off a top-priority creditor you'll move the othe up the ladder for their turn at #1. **If you stay disciplined**, always rolling your previous payments into your new top-priority, you'll be delighted at how powerfully this strategy leads you to Debt-Freeland.

When that magic moment arrives, birds will sing and flowers bloom. A rainbow will span your financial horizon. **The revolving door will finally stop** and let you out—out to breathe deeply and spread your wings. **Now you can redirect those debt-servicing dollars to saving, giving, and debt-free *fun***. You are free at last, free at last, thank God Almighty, free at last.

Guiding Principle 1

Avoid using credit for items that are perishable or that depreciate in value.

Guiding Principle 2

Get interest working FOR you. Convert your consumer debt into increased savings and investments.

Guiding Principle 3

The best way to get something done is to begin.

Guiding Principle 4

Now, STAY debt-free.

The financial world has invented dozens of convenient ways to pull you back into the revolving door. Perhaps most annoying is *an unsolicited supply of blank checks* your mailbox, courtesy of your credit card company, with your name and address already imprinted.

Shred.

To Keep Credit Spending Under Control...

- **Stick to the One Card Only rule**. That's all you'll need from here on. Shred all invitations for additional cards.

- **Ask yourself some tough questions**. When the urge for unplanned credit-card spending rears its seductive head (and it will), ask yourself: "*REALLY? Is this a whim I'll regret in a week? Will I want this item as badly in thirty days when the bill comes?*"

- **If you do use your One Card Only, pay it off in full when the statement arrives**. If you slip back into the pattern of not paying in full at the end of each month, bring on the scissors and use only a debit card.
- **Avoid future debt and finance charges by saving in advance for major purchases**. Now that you've converted all your debt-servicing dollars into savings dollars, you can save in advance for future needs and dreams.

• Above all, BE BOLD

and

STAND STRONG.

IT'S WORTH THE EFFORT!

This Pocket Plan has shown you how to escape and stay clear of the debt trap. Is it worth the effort? You bet. Can you do it? Absolutely. Should you? Hey, we're talking financial freedom here!

KEEP THE GOAL IN SIGHT

When you keep consumer debt under control...

- You'll feel a greater sense of security, control, and peace of mind.

- You won't feel so "strapped" between paychecks.

- You'll have more discretionary dollars, enabling you to purchase with cash instead of expensive credit.

- You'll build a savings reserve to cover true emergencies and pay-as-you-go for vacations or other major purchases.
- You'll be able to invest more diligently for the long term so you'll be financially independent when retirement comes.
- Most importantly, you'll be able to give more to your church, to a worthy ministry, charity, or to someone in need.

And we're not just thinking "years down the road." Blast away at debt, stay true to your resolve, and you'll begin reaping the rewards right away. You will truly understand what we mean when we emphasize: ***Get rid of consumer debt—for good***.

Additional copies of this and other
Honor products are available wherever good books are sold.

If you have enjoyed this book,
or if it has had an impact on your life,
we would like to hear from you.

Please contact us at:
Honor Books
Cook Communications Ministries, Dept. 201
4050 Lee Vance View
Colorado Springs, CO 80918
Or visit our Web site:
www.cookministries.com

HONOR **B** BOOKS

Inspiration and Motivation for the Seasons of Life